# THE WEALTH BLUEPRINT: MASTERING FINANCIAL SUCCESS

*The Wealth Blueprint*

## Rahad Pramanik

**Rahad**

ISBN-13: 9798884390003
ISBN-10: 1477123456

Cover design by: Art Painter
Library of Congress Control Number: 2018675309
Printed in the United States of America

# THE WEALTH BLUEPRINT: MASTERING FINANCIAL SUCCESS

## Book Chapters:

- Setting Your Financial Goals
- Building a Solid Budget Plan
- Investing Wisely for Long-Term Growth
- Understanding and Managing Debt
- The Power of Passive Income Streams
- Real Estate Investment Strategies
- Navigating the Stock Market with Confidence
- Entrepreneurship and Business Ventures
- Retirement Planning and Wealth Preservation
- Tax Strategies for Maximizing Returns
- Wealth Protection and Insurance Planning
- Estate Planning for Generational Wealth
- Mastering the Mindset of Financial Success
- Overcoming Financial Challenges and Setbacks
- Creating a Legacy of Financial Freedom

## Book Introduction:

Welcome to "The Wealth Blueprint: Mastering Financial Success." In this comprehensive guide, we delve into the intricacies of achieving and maintaining financial prosperity. From setting clear financial goals to navigating the complexities of investment vehicles, this book is designed to equip you with the knowledge and tools necessary to build and preserve wealth.

With over 15 chapters covering a wide array of financial topics, you'll learn practical strategies for budgeting, investing, debt management, passive income generation, and much more. Whether you're just starting on your financial journey or seeking to enhance your existing wealth-building strategies, this book offers actionable insights tailored to individuals at every stage of their financial lives.

Prepare to embark on a transformative journey towards financial empowerment and abundance. By implementing the principles outlined in these pages, you'll pave the way towards a future of financial freedom and fulfilment.

# CHAPTER 1: SETTING YOUR FINANCIAL GOALS:

 Embarking on a journey to financial success begins with clarity of purpose and vision. In this chapter, we explore the importance of setting specific, measurable, achievable, relevant, and time-bound (SMART) financial goals. Whether your aspirations involve purchasing a home, starting a business, or retiring comfortably, articulating your objectives lays the foundation for effective wealth planning.

To begin, take time to reflect on your long-term aspirations and values. What do you hope to accomplish financially in the next five, ten, or twenty years? By aligning your financial goals with your personal values and priorities, you'll derive greater motivation and commitment towards achieving them.

Once you've identified your overarching objectives, break them down into smaller, actionable steps. This process not only makes your goals more manageable but also allows for regular progress tracking and adjustments as needed. Whether it's saving a specific amount each month, paying off debt, or increasing your investment contributions, establishing concrete action plans is key to success.

Moreover, consider the potential obstacles and challenges that may arise along the way. Anticipating setbacks allows you to devise contingency plans and stay resilient in the face of adversity. Remember, setbacks are not failures but opportunities for growth and course correction.

In essence, setting your financial goals is the crucial first step towards realizing your dreams. By defining clear objectives, developing actionable plans, and remaining adaptable in the pursuit of success, you'll lay a solid foundation for a future of financial abundance and fulfilment.

# CHAPTER 2: BUILDING A SOLID BUDGET PLAN

Managing your finances effectively begins with establishing a robust budget plan. In this chapter, we'll explore the fundamental principles of budgeting and provide practical strategies for creating a budget that aligns with your financial goals.

To begin, it's essential to track your income and expenses diligently. Take inventory of all sources of income, including salaries, bonuses, investments, and any other sources of revenue. Next, analyze your expenses by categorizing them into essential (such as housing, food, and utilities) and discretionary (such as entertainment, dining out, and shopping).

Once you have a clear understanding of your income and expenses, it's time to create a budget that balances your financial priorities. Allocate a portion of your income towards essential expenses, ensuring that you cover necessities while still leaving room for savings and discretionary spending. Aim to save at least 10-20% of your income for future goals and emergencies.

When crafting your budget, don't forget to factor in irregular expenses and occasional bills, such as insurance premiums, taxes, and maintenance costs. Set aside funds each month to cover these expenses, either through a dedicated savings account or by allocating a portion of your discretionary spending.

Moreover, consider using budgeting tools and apps to streamline the process and track your progress over time. Many apps offer features such as expense categorization, goal tracking, and real-time spending alerts, making it easier to stay on top of your finances.

Lastly, remember that budgeting is not a one-time task but an ongoing process. Review and adjust your budget regularly to reflect changes in your income, expenses, and financial goals. By staying proactive and disciplined in your budgeting efforts, you'll cultivate financial stability and resilience for the long term.

In summary, building a solid budget plan is essential for managing your finances effectively and achieving your financial goals. By tracking your income and expenses, allocating funds strategically, and leveraging technology to streamline the process, you'll lay the groundwork for a future of financial success and security.

# CHAPTER 3: INVESTING WISELY FOR LONG-TERM GROWTH

Investing is a cornerstone of wealth building, providing the opportunity for long-term growth and financial security. In this chapter, we'll delve into the principles of wise investing and explore various investment strategies to help you achieve your financial objectives.

Before diving into specific investment options, it's crucial to understand your risk tolerance, investment timeframe, and financial goals. Are you comfortable with taking on higher risk for the potential of greater returns, or do you prefer more conservative investments with lower volatility? Additionally, consider your investment horizon—are you investing for the short term, such as buying a house, or for the long term, such as retirement?

Once you've assessed your risk tolerance and investment timeframe, it's time to construct a diversified investment portfolio. Diversification is key to reducing risk and maximizing returns over time. Spread your investments across different asset classes, such as stocks, bonds, real estate, and alternative investments, to mitigate the impact of market fluctuations.

When selecting specific investments, consider factors such as historical performance, fees, and potential for growth. For stocks, research companies with strong fundamentals, competitive advantages, and growth potential. For bonds, evaluate credit quality, yield, and maturity dates. Real estate investments can offer passive income and appreciation potential, while alternative investments like commodities and cryptocurrencies can provide diversification benefits.

Moreover, don't underestimate the power of compounding and regular contributions. By investing consistently over time, you can harness the power of compound interest to grow your wealth exponentially. Set up automatic contributions to your investment accounts and reinvest dividends to maximize your returns.

Finally, stay informed and educated about the financial markets and investment trends. Keep abreast of economic indicators, market news, and regulatory changes that may impact your investments. Consider consulting with a financial advisor to develop a personalized investment strategy tailored to your goals and risk profile.

In summary, investing wisely is essential for long-term wealth accumulation and financial success. By understanding your risk tolerance, diversifying your portfolio, and staying disciplined in your investment approach, you can build a solid foundation for a prosperous future.

# CHAPTER 4: UNDERSTANDING AND MANAGING DEBT

Debt can be a double-edged sword—it can facilitate important purchases and investments, but it can also become a burden if not managed properly. In this chapter, we'll explore the types of debt, strategies for managing debt  effectively, and steps to reduce debt over time.

Firstly, it's essential to distinguish between good debt and bad debt. Good debt typically refers to borrowing for investments that have the potential to increase in value or generate income, such as student loans for education or a mortgage for a home. Bad debt, on the other hand, includes high-interest consumer debt used to finance discretionary purchases, such as credit card debt or payday loans.

To manage debt effectively, start by assessing your current debt situation. Make a list of all your outstanding debts, including balances, interest rates, and minimum monthly payments. This will give you a clear picture of your total debt load and help prioritize repayment efforts.

Next, develop a debt repayment strategy that aligns with your financial goals and budget. Consider using the debt snowball or debt avalanche method to prioritize repayment. With the snowball method, you focus on paying off the smallest debt first, then move on to the next smallest debt, and so on, gaining momentum as you eliminate each debt. The avalanche method, on the other hand, prioritizes paying off debts with the highest interest rates first to minimize interest costs over time.

Additionally, explore opportunities to refinance or consolidate high-interest debt to lower your interest rates and simplify repayment. Balance transfer credit cards, personal loans, or home equity loans may offer lower interest rates and more favourable repayment terms, allowing you to pay off debt more efficiently.

While prioritizing debt repayment, don't neglect other financial goals such as saving for emergencies or investing for the future. Strike a balance between debt repayment and saving to ensure long-term financial stability.

Finally, take proactive steps to avoid accumulating new debt in the future. Practice responsible spending habits, avoid unnecessary purchases, and build an emergency fund to cover unexpected expenses without resorting to borrowing.

In summary, understanding and managing debt is essential for achieving financial freedom and security. By assessing your debt situation, developing a repayment strategy, and adopting responsible financial habits, you can take control of your finances and pave the way towards a debt-free future.

# CHAPTER 5: THE POWER OF PASSIVE INCOME STREAMS

Passive income streams offer a pathway to financial independence by generating income with minimal ongoing effort or active involvement. In this chapter, we'll explore various passive income opportunities and strategies for building multiple streams of passive income.

Passive income can take many forms, including rental income from real estate properties, dividends from stocks and mutual funds, interest from savings accounts and bonds, royalties from creative works or intellectual property, and income generated from online businesses or affiliate marketing.

One of the most popular forms of passive income is real estate investing. By purchasing rental properties and leasing them to tenants, investors can generate a steady stream of rental income while potentially benefiting from property appreciation over time. Real estate crowdfunding platforms also offer opportunities to invest in real estate projects with lower capital requirements and reduced management responsibilities.

Dividend investing involves purchasing stocks of companies

that regularly pay dividends to shareholders. By building a diversified portfolio of dividend-paying stocks, investors can earn passive income through regular dividend payments, which can be reinvested for compounded growth or used as supplemental income.

Interest income from savings accounts, certificates of deposit (CDs), and bonds provides another avenue for generating passive income. While interest rates may be relatively low in today's low-rate environment, these investments can still provide a stable source of income with minimal risk.

Moreover, creative individuals can generate passive income through royalties from books, music, art, and other creative works. By licensing their creations to third parties or self-publishing through platforms like Amazon Kindle Direct Publishing, creators can earn ongoing royalties from sales and usage rights.

Finally, the internet has opened up a world of opportunities for building passive income streams through online businesses, affiliate marketing, and content creation. Websites, blogs, YouTube channels, and social media platforms can all be monetized through advertising, sponsorships, affiliate partnerships, and digital product sales.

In summary, passive income streams offer a powerful means of achieving financial freedom and autonomy. By diversifying your income sources and leveraging opportunities in real estate, dividend investing, interest income, royalties, and online businesses, you can build multiple streams of passive income to support your financial goals and aspirations.

# CHAPTER 6: REAL ESTATE INVESTMENT STRATEGIES

Real estate investment offers a tangible and potentially lucrative opportunity for building wealth over the long term. In this chapter, we'll explore various real estate investment strategies, from rental properties to real estate investment trusts (REITs) and provide practical tips for success in the real estate market.

One of the most common real estate investment strategies is purchasing rental properties. By acquiring residential or commercial properties and leasing them to tenants, investors can generate rental income while potentially benefiting from property appreciation over time. Successful rental property investing requires careful property selection, diligent tenant screening, and effective property management to maximize returns and minimize risks.

Another approach to real estate investment is flipping properties. Flipping involves purchasing properties below market value, renovating or improving them, and selling them for a profit. While flipping can be profitable, it also carries higher risks and requires expertise in property valuation, renovation, and market analysis to succeed.

For investors seeking a more passive approach to real estate investing, real estate investment trusts (REITs) offer an attractive option. REITs are companies that own, operate, or finance income-producing real estate properties. By investing in REITs, investors can gain exposure to a diversified portfolio of real estate assets without the hassle of property management. REITs typically distribute a significant portion of their income to shareholders in the form of dividends, making them an attractive option for income-oriented investors.

Moreover, crowdfunding platforms have emerged as a popular way to invest in real estate with lower capital requirements and reduced barriers to entry. Real estate crowdfunding allows investors to pool their funds to invest in real estate projects, such as residential developments, commercial properties, or multifamily housing, and earn returns based on the performance of the underlying assets.

In summary, real estate investment offers a myriad of opportunities for building wealth and achieving financial independence. Whether through rental properties, property flipping, REITs, or crowdfunding platforms, investors can leverage real estate to generate passive income, build equity, and diversify their investment portfolios. With careful research, due diligence, and strategic planning, real estate can be a rewarding avenue for long-term wealth creation.

# CHAPTER 7: NAVIGATING THE STOCK MARKET WITH CONFIDENCE

Investing in the stock market can be an excellent way to grow your wealth over time, but it requires knowledge, patience, and a disciplined approach. In this chapter, we'll discuss strategies for navigating the 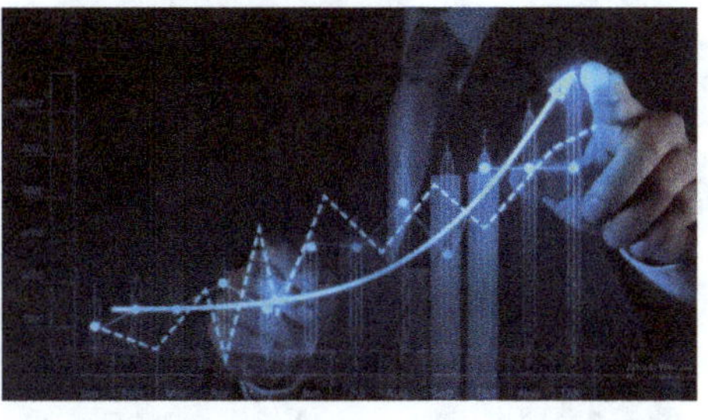 stock market with confidence and achieving long-term investment success.

Before diving into the stock market, it's essential to understand the basics of investing and familiarize yourself with key investment principles. This includes understanding the concept of risk and return, diversification, and the importance of investing for the long term. Additionally, take time to educate yourself about different investment vehicles, such as individual stocks, mutual funds, exchange-traded funds (ETFs), and index funds.

Once you've laid the groundwork, develop a well-defined investment strategy that aligns with your financial goals, risk tolerance, and investment timeframe. Determine your asset allocation—that is, how much of your portfolio you'll allocate to stocks, bonds, and other asset classes—and rebalance your portfolio periodically to maintain your desired risk-return profile.

When selecting individual stocks, focus on companies with strong fundamentals, competitive advantages, and sustainable growth prospects. Conduct thorough research into the company's financial performance, business model, management team, and industry dynamics before making investment decisions. Consider factors such as revenue growth, earnings stability, profitability, and valuation metrics to assess the company's investment potential.

Moreover, practice disciplined portfolio management by diversifying your investments across different sectors, industries, and geographic regions to reduce risk and maximize returns. Avoid making impulsive investment decisions based on market fluctuations or short-term trends, and instead, stay focused on your long-term investment objectives.

Additionally, consider investing in index funds or ETFs to gain broad exposure to the stock market while minimizing individual stock risk. These passively managed investment vehicles replicate the performance of a market index, such as the S&P 500, and offer low fees and broad diversification.

Finally, stay informed about market trends, economic indicators, and company-specific news that may impact your investments. However, avoid becoming overly influenced by short-term market fluctuations or speculative noise, and maintain a long-term perspective on your investments.

In summary, navigating the stock market with confidence requires a solid understanding of investment principles, a well-defined investment strategy, and disciplined portfolio management. By focusing on fundamentals, maintaining a diversified portfolio, and staying committed to your long-term goals, you can navigate the ups and downs of the stock market and achieve investment success over time.

# CHAPTER 8: ENTREPRENEURSHIP AND BUSINESS VENTURES

Entrepreneurship presents an exciting opportunity to build wealth and create value by bringing innovative ideas to market. In this chapter, we'll explore the fundamentals of entrepreneurship, discuss strategies for launching and growing a successful business venture, and highlight key considerations for aspiring entrepreneurs.

Entrepreneurship is not just about starting a business—it's about identifying unmet needs or inefficiencies in the market and developing solutions to address them. Successful entrepreneurs possess a combination of creativity, resilience, adaptability, and a willingness to take calculated risks.

To embark on the entrepreneurial journey, start by identifying your passion, interests, and areas of expertise. What problems or challenges are you uniquely positioned to solve? Conduct market research to validate your business idea and assess demand, competition, and potential profitability.

Once you've identified a viable business opportunity, develop a comprehensive business plan outlining your vision, mission, target market, value proposition, marketing strategy, operational plan, and financial projections. A well-crafted business plan serves as a roadmap for your venture and helps attract investors, partners, and stakeholders.

Next, focus on building a strong team of talented individuals who share your vision and complement your skills. Surround yourself with advisors, mentors, and experts who can provide guidance, support, and valuable insights as you navigate the complexities of entrepreneurship.

Moreover, leverage technology and innovation to streamline operations, reach customers, and differentiate your business in the marketplace. Embrace digital marketing, e-commerce platforms, and social media to connect with your target audience and drive sales.

As your business grows, prioritize customer satisfaction, innovation, and continuous improvement to maintain a competitive edge and sustain long-term success. Stay agile and adaptable in response to changing market dynamics, customer preferences, and industry trends.

Finally, manage your finances prudently and seek funding sources that align with your business needs and growth objectives. Whether through bootstrapping, crowdfunding, venture capital, or small business loans, secure the necessary capital to fuel your business growth while minimizing financial risks.

In summary, entrepreneurship offers a pathway to financial independence and personal fulfillment by turning ideas into reality and creating value in the marketplace. By embracing creativity, resilience, and strategic thinking, aspiring entrepreneurs can launch and grow successful business ventures that make a positive impact on society and generate wealth for themselves and their stakeholders.

# CHAPTER 9: RETIREMENT PLANNING AND WEALTH PRESERVATION

Planning for retirement is a critical aspect of achieving long-term financial security and peace of mind. In this chapter, we'll discuss the importance of retirement planning, explore strategies for building a retirement nest egg, and  highlight key considerations for preserving wealth throughout retirement.

Retirement planning involves setting financial goals, estimating retirement expenses, and developing a savings and investment strategy to fund your desired lifestyle during retirement. Start by assessing your current financial situation, including your income, expenses, assets, and liabilities. Determine your retirement goals, such as the age at which you wish to retire and the lifestyle you envision during retirement.

Next, estimate your retirement expenses, including housing, healthcare, transportation, leisure activities, and other living costs. Consider factors such as inflation, healthcare expenses, and potential long-term care needs when projecting your retirement expenses.

Once you have a clear understanding of your retirement goals and expenses, develop a savings and investment plan to accumulate the necessary funds for retirement. Take advantage of tax-advantaged retirement accounts such as 401(k)s, IRAs, and Roth IRAs to maximize your savings potential and minimize your tax liability.

Invest your retirement savings in a diversified portfolio of assets tailored to your risk tolerance, investment timeframe, and retirement goals. Consider a mix of stocks, bonds, mutual funds, and other investment vehicles to balance risk and return and achieve your desired investment outcomes.

Moreover, consider incorporating guaranteed income sources into your retirement plan, such as Social Security benefits, pensions, annuities, and other sources of lifetime income. These sources can provide a reliable stream of income to supplement your retirement savings and cover essential expenses during retirement.

As you approach retirement, shift your investment focus from growth-oriented investments to wealth preservation strategies aimed at protecting your retirement assets and generating a sustainable income stream. Consider strategies such as asset allocation, tax-efficient withdrawal strategies, and long-term care planning to safeguard your wealth and ensure financial stability in retirement.

Finally, periodically review and adjust your retirement plan as needed to account for changes in your financial situation, lifestyle preferences, and economic conditions. Stay informed about retirement planning best practices, regulatory changes, and investment trends to make informed decisions and maximize your retirement outcomes.

In summary, retirement planning is a lifelong process that requires careful consideration, diligent saving and investing, and ongoing monitoring and adjustment. By taking proactive steps to build a retirement nest egg, preserve wealth, and adapt to changing circumstances, you can enjoy a financially secure and fulfilling retirement journey.

# CHAPTER 10: TAX STRATEGIES FOR MAXIMIZING RETURNS

Understanding and optimizing your tax strategy is crucial for maximizing your investment returns and preserving wealth over the long term. In this chapter, we'll explore various tax-saving strategies and techniques to help you minimize your tax liability and keep more of your hard-earned money.

One of the most effective tax-saving strategies is taking advantage of tax-advantaged retirement accounts, such as 401(k)s, IRAs, and Roth IRAs. Contributions to these accounts are typically tax-deductible or tax-deferred, allowing you to reduce your taxable income and grow your investments tax-free until retirement. Consider maximizing your contributions to these accounts each year to take full advantage of their tax benefits.

Additionally, consider utilizing tax-loss harvesting to offset capital gains and reduce your tax liability. Tax-loss harvesting involves selling investments that have experienced a loss and using those losses to offset capital gains realized from other investments. By strategically harvesting losses, you can reduce your taxable income and potentially lower your overall tax bill.

Moreover, explore opportunities to invest in tax-efficient investment vehicles, such as index funds, exchange-traded funds (ETFs), and municipal bonds. These investments are structured to minimize taxable distributions and capital gains, allowing you to keep more of your investment returns and reduce your tax burden over time.

Consider leveraging tax-deferred growth vehicles, such as annuities and cash value life insurance, to defer taxes on investment gains and grow your wealth more efficiently. While these vehicles may come with fees and restrictions, they can provide valuable tax advantages for high-income earners and individuals seeking to maximize their tax-deferred savings potential.

Furthermore, be mindful of tax-efficient withdrawal strategies during retirement to minimize the tax impact of your distributions. Consider strategies such as Roth IRA conversions, systematic withdrawals, and managing your taxable income to optimize your tax situation and maximize your retirement income.

Finally, work with a qualified tax advisor or financial planner to develop a personalized tax strategy tailored to your financial goals, investment portfolio, and tax situation. A knowledgeable advisor can help you navigate complex tax laws, identify tax-saving opportunities, and implement strategies to minimize your tax liability effectively.

In summary, tax planning is an integral part of wealth management and investment strategy. By implementing tax-efficient investment vehicles, leveraging tax-advantaged accounts, and utilizing tax-saving strategies, you can minimize your tax liability, maximize your investment returns, and preserve more of your wealth for the future.

# CHAPTER 11: WEALTH PROTECTION AND INSURANCE PLANNING

Protecting your wealth and assets from unexpected risks is essential for preserving your financial security and achieving long-term prosperity. In this chapter, we'll explore the importance of wealth protection, discuss various insurance options, and provide strategies for mitigating risks effectively.

Wealth protection involves identifying potential risks and implementing strategies to safeguard your assets against unforeseen events such as accidents, illness, disability, lawsuits, and natural disasters. By proactively addressing these risks, you can protect your financial well-being and minimize the impact of adverse events on your wealth.

One of the foundational pillars of wealth protection is insurance planning. Insurance provides a safety net against financial losses by transferring risk to an insurance company in exchange for a premium. There are several types of insurance policies that individuals can consider protecting their assets and loved ones:

- **Health Insurance:** Health insurance covers medical expenses and provides financial protection against healthcare costs arising from illness, injury, or medical treatments. Choose a health insurance plan that meets your needs and budget, considering factors such as coverage options, premiums, deductibles, and out-of-pocket expenses.

- **Life Insurance:** Life insurance provides financial protection for your loved ones in the event of your death. There are various types of life insurance policies, including term life insurance, whole life insurance, and universal life insurance. Evaluate your life insurance needs based on factors such as your age, income, family obligations, and financial goals.

- **Disability Insurance:** Disability insurance provides income replacement if you become unable to work due to illness or injury. It helps cover living expenses, medical bills, and other financial obligations during periods of disability. Consider purchasing both short-term and long-term disability insurance to protect your income and financial stability.

- **Property and Casualty Insurance:** Property and casualty insurance, including homeowners' insurance, renters' insurance, and auto insurance, protects against damage or loss of property and liability for accidents or injuries. Review your insurance coverage regularly to ensure adequate protection against property damage, theft, natural disasters, and liability claims.

- **Umbrella Insurance:** Umbrella insurance provides additional liability coverage beyond the limits of your primary insurance policies. It offers protection against lawsuits and legal claims that exceed the coverage limits of your homeowners, auto, or other liability insurance policies.

In addition to insurance planning, consider implementing risk management strategies to mitigate other potential threats to your wealth. This may include establishing legal structures such as trusts, LLCs, or asset protection strategies to shield your assets from creditors, lawsuits, or other claims.

Moreover, maintain an emergency fund to cover unexpected expenses and financial setbacks, such as job loss, medical emergencies, or major home repairs. Aim to save at least three to six months' worth of living expenses in a readily accessible savings account or cash reserve.

Finally, regularly review and update your wealth protection strategies in response to changes in your financial situation, lifestyle, and risk profile. Work with a qualified financial advisor or insurance agent to assess your insurance needs, explore coverage options, and tailor a comprehensive wealth protection plan that meets your specific requirements.

In summary, wealth protection is a critical component of financial planning and risk management. By implementing insurance planning, risk mitigation strategies, and emergency preparedness measures, you can safeguard your assets, protect your financial well-being, and achieve greater peace of mind in the face of life's uncertainties.

# CHAPTER 12: ESTATE PLANNING FOR GENERATIONAL WEALTH

Estate planning is a vital component of comprehensive wealth management, ensuring that your assets are preserved and transferred to your heirs according to your wishes. In this chapter, we'll explore the importance of estate planning, discuss key components of an estate plan, and provide strategies for preserving generational wealth.

Estate planning involves the process of organizing your affairs and making decisions about how your assets will be managed and distributed upon your death or incapacitation. Regardless of the size of your estate, having a well-thought-out estate plan can help minimize taxes, avoid probate, and provide for your loved ones' financial security.

One of the central elements of estate planning is creating a will—a legal document that specifies how your assets will be distributed after your death. In your will, you can designate beneficiaries for your assets, appoint guardians for minor children, and name an executor to oversee the administration of your estate.

In addition to a will, consider establishing a trust to manage and distribute your assets according to your wishes. Trusts offer greater flexibility, privacy, and control over the distribution of assets, and can help avoid the probate process, which can be costly and time-consuming.

Moreover, review and update your beneficiary designations regularly to ensure they reflect your current wishes and circumstances. Retirement accounts, life insurance policies, and other financial accounts typically allow you to designate beneficiaries who will receive the assets upon your death. By keeping these designations current, you can avoid unintended consequences and ensure that your assets are distributed according to your wishes.

Another critical aspect of estate planning is minimizing estate taxes and maximizing the amount of wealth transferred to your heirs. This may involve leveraging estate planning tools and techniques such as gifting, charitable giving, and estate tax planning strategies to reduce the tax burden on your estate and preserve more wealth for future generations.

Furthermore, consider planning for incapacity by establishing powers of attorney and healthcare directives that designate trusted individuals to make financial and medical decisions on your behalf if you become incapacitated. These documents ensure that your wishes are respected, and your affairs are managed effectively in the event of illness or incapacity.

Finally, involve your family members in the estate planning process and communicate your wishes openly and transparently. Discussing your estate plan with your loved ones can help avoid misunderstandings, conflicts, and legal disputes down the road and ensure a smooth transition of assets to the next generation.

In summary, estate planning is essential for preserving generational wealth, protecting your assets, and ensuring that your wishes are carried out after your death. By creating a comprehensive estate plan that includes a will, trusts, beneficiary designations, and incapacity planning documents, you can provide for your loved ones' financial security and leave a legacy for future generations.

# CHAPTER 13: MASTERING THE MINDSET OF FINANCIAL SUCCESS

Achieving financial success is not only about implementing sound strategies and tactics but also cultivating the right mindset and attitudes towards money and wealth. In this chapter, we'll explore the key principles and mindset shifts that can help you master the mindset of financial success and achieve your financial goals.

- **Abundance Mindset:** Adopting an abundance mindset involves believing that there are ample opportunities for wealth and prosperity in the world. Instead of viewing wealth as a finite resource, embrace the belief that you can create abundance in your life through hard work, creativity, and perseverance.

- **Financial Education:** Commit to lifelong learning and continuous improvement in your financial knowledge and skills. Educate yourself about personal finance, investing, entrepreneurship, and wealth-building strategies through books, courses, seminars, and other resources. The more you know about money and how it works, the better equipped you'll be to make informed financial decisions and achieve your goals.

- **Goal Setting:** Set clear, specific, and achievable financial goals that align with your values, priorities, and aspirations.

Whether it's saving for retirement, buying a home, starting a business, or paying off debt, articulate your goals and develop actionable plans to achieve them. Break down larger goals into smaller, manageable tasks and celebrate your progress along the way.

- **Delayed Gratification:** Practice delayed gratification by prioritizing long-term financial goals over short-term pleasures and instant gratification. Avoid impulse spending, unnecessary debt, and lifestyle inflation that can derail your financial progress. Instead, focus on making intentional choices that align with your long-term financial objectives and values.

- **Risk-Taking and Resilience:** Embrace risk-taking as an essential aspect of wealth-building and entrepreneurship. Understand that taking calculated risks is necessary for growth and innovation and be willing to step outside your comfort zone to pursue opportunities for financial success. Moreover, cultivate resilience and perseverance to overcome setbacks, failures, and obstacles along the way. View challenges as opportunities for growth and learning and stay committed to your financial goals despite temporary setbacks.

- **Gratitude and Generosity:** Cultivate gratitude for the resources and opportunities you have, and practice generosity by giving back to others and supporting causes you care about. Recognize the importance of wealth not only for personal fulfilment but also for making a positive impact on the lives of others and contributing to the greater good.

- **Financial Independence:** Strive for financial independence— the ability to sustain your desired lifestyle without relying on a paycheck or external sources of income. Achieving financial independence grants you the freedom to pursue your passions, follow your dreams, and live life on your own terms, without being beholden to financial constraints or obligations.

By embracing these principles and adopting a mindset of financial success, you can empower yourself to take control of your financial future, overcome challenges, and achieve your most ambitious goals. Remember that financial success is not just about accumulating wealth but also about living a fulfilling, purpose-driven life aligned with your values and aspirations.

# CHAPTER 14: CULTIVATING HEALTHY FINANCIAL HABITS

Building wealth and achieving financial success is not just about making the right decisions—it's also about cultivating healthy financial habits that support your goals and aspirations. In this chapter, we'll explore essential financial habits that can help you take control of your finances, build wealth, and achieve long-term prosperity.

- **Budgeting and Tracking Expenses:** Establish a budget that aligns with your financial goals and priorities and track your expenses regularly to ensure that you're living within your means. Use budgeting tools, apps, or spreadsheets to monitor your income, expenses, and savings, and adjust as needed to stay on track.
- **Saving and Investing:** Cultivate a habit of saving and investing regularly to build wealth over time. Pay yourself first by automating savings contributions from your pay check or bank account and allocate a portion of your income towards long-term investments such as retirement accounts, brokerage accounts, or real estate properties.
- **Living Below Your Means:** Practice living below your means by spending less than you earn and avoiding unnecessary debt and frivolous expenses. Adopt a minimalist mindset and

prioritize experiences and meaningful purchases over material possessions and seek out ways to reduce expenses and increase savings wherever possible.

- **Emergency Fund:** Build an emergency fund to cover unexpected expenses and financial setbacks, such as job loss, medical emergencies, or major home repairs. Aim to save at least three to six months' worth of living expenses in a readily accessible savings account or cash reserve to provide a financial cushion in times of need.
- **Debt Management:** Take a proactive approach to managing debt by paying off high-interest debt aggressively and avoiding new debt whenever possible. Develop a debt repayment plan that prioritizes high-interest debts first and consider consolidating or refinancing loans to lower interest rates and streamline repayment.
- **Continuous Learning:** Invest in your financial education and personal development by reading books, attending workshops, and seeking guidance from financial advisors or mentors. Stay informed about personal finance topics, investment strategies, and economic trends to make informed decisions and adapt to changing circumstances.
- **Long-Term Planning:** Develop a long-term financial plan that encompasses your goals, values, and aspirations for the future. Consider factors such as retirement planning, education funding, estate planning, and legacy planning to ensure that your financial affairs are structured to support your desired lifestyle and provide for your loved ones.
- **Regular Review and Adjustment:** Regularly review and adjust your financial habits, goals, and strategies in response to changes in your life circumstances, financial situation, and economic conditions. Stay flexible and adaptable and be willing to make course corrections as needed to stay on track towards your financial objectives.

By cultivating healthy financial habits and incorporating them into your daily routine, you can build a solid foundation for financial success and achieve your long-term goals with confidence and peace of mind. Remember that financial success is a journey, not a destination, and that small, consistent actions taken over time can lead to significant results.

# CHAPTER 15: EMBRACING FINANCIAL INDEPENDENCE

Financial independence is the goal for many individuals seeking freedom, flexibility, and control over their lives. In this chapter, we'll explore the concept of financial independence, discuss strategies for achieving it, and highlight the benefits of living a life free from financial constraints.

Financial independence is the state of being able to cover your living expenses and achieve your desired lifestyle without relying on a traditional job or external sources of income. It grants you the freedom to pursue your passions, interests, and goals without being constrained by financial obligations or limitations.

To achieve financial independence, focus on increasing your income, reducing expenses, and building passive income streams that generate enough revenue to cover your living expenses. Invest in assets that appreciate over time, such as stocks, real estate, and business ventures, and leverage the power of compound interest to grow your wealth exponentially.

Moreover, live below your means and prioritize saving and investing a significant portion of your income towards long-term financial goals. Adopt frugal habits, avoid lifestyle inflation, and seek out ways to reduce expenses and increase savings wherever possible. The more you can save and invest now, the faster you can achieve financial independence and enjoy the benefits of financial freedom.

Consider diversifying your income streams and exploring alternative sources of passive income, such as rental properties, dividend-paying stocks, online businesses, and royalties from creative works. Multiple streams of passive income can provide a reliable source of cash flow and reduce reliance on a single source of income, increasing financial resilience and stability.

Moreover, focus on building assets that provide both financial and personal fulfilment, such as pursuing entrepreneurship, investing in projects aligned with your passions and values, and creating meaningful experiences that enrich your life and contribute to your overall well-being.

Ultimately, financial independence is not just about accumulating wealth—it's about designing a life that aligns with your values, priorities, and aspirations. It's about having the freedom to spend your time and resources in ways that bring you joy, fulfilment, and purpose, without being bound by financial constraints or obligations.

By embracing the principles of financial independence, living intentionally, and aligning your financial decisions with your values and goals, you can create a life of abundance, fulfilment, and freedom. Whether you choose to retire early, pursue your passions, travel the world, or give back to your community, financial independence empowers you to live life on your own terms and create a legacy that extends far beyond your financial assets.

# CHAPTER 16: MINDFUL SPENDING AND CONSCIOUS CONSUMPTION

In today's consumer-driven society, it's easy to fall into the trap of mindless spending and excessive consumption. In this chapter, we'll explore the concept of mindful spending and conscious consumption, and how adopting these practices can lead to greater financial well-being and personal fulfillment.

Mindful spending involves being intentional and deliberate about how you allocate your financial resources. It's about aligning your spending with your values, priorities, and long-term goals, rather than succumbing to impulse purchases or societal pressures. By practicing mindful spending, you can cultivate a deeper appreciation for your purchases, reduce wasteful spending, and make more meaningful choices that contribute to your overall well-being.

Conscious consumption goes hand in hand with mindful spending, emphasizing the importance of considering the ethical, environmental, and social impact of your purchasing decisions. It involves questioning the necessity of purchases, researching companies and products to ensure they align with your values, and supporting businesses that prioritize sustainability, social responsibility, and ethical practices. By practicing conscious consumption, you can minimize your environmental footprint, support causes you believe in, and contribute to positive social change through your purchasing power.

In this chapter, we'll explore practical strategies for incorporating mindful spending and conscious consumption into your daily life, such as creating a budget based on your values, tracking your spending habits, practicing gratitude for what you have, and seeking out alternative ways to meet your needs that align with your values and priorities. By adopting these practices, you can cultivate a more mindful and intentional approach to spending and consumption, leading to greater financial security, personal fulfillment, and environmental sustainability.

# CHAPTER 17: NAVIGATING ECONOMIC UNCERTAINTY

Economic uncertainty is an inevitable part of life, with fluctuating market conditions, geopolitical events, and unforeseen crises contributing to financial instability. In this chapter, we'll explore strategies for navigating economic uncertainty and safeguarding your financial well-being in the face of volatility and upheaval.

First and foremost, it's essential to maintain a long-term perspective and resist the temptation to react impulsively to short-term market fluctuations or economic downturns. Instead of trying to time the market or predict future events, focus on building a diversified investment portfolio that can withstand various economic scenarios and generate consistent returns over time.

Additionally, establish an emergency fund to cover unexpected expenses and financial setbacks, such as job loss, medical emergencies, or market downturns. Aim to save at least three to six months' worth of living expenses in a readily accessible savings account or cash reserve to provide a financial cushion in times of need.

Furthermore, stay informed about economic trends, market developments, and geopolitical events that could impact your investments or financial situation. Keep abreast of news and analysis from reputable sources, consult with financial professionals, and consider adjusting your investment strategy or asset allocation as needed to adapt to changing economic conditions.

Moreover, focus on controlling what you can control, such as your spending habits, savings rate, and investment strategy, rather than worrying about factors beyond your control. By taking proactive steps to strengthen your financial position, you can minimize the impact of economic uncertainty and position yourself for long-term success, regardless of external conditions.

In summary, navigating economic uncertainty requires a combination of preparedness, resilience, and adaptability. By staying informed, maintaining a long-term perspective, and taking proactive steps to safeguard your financial well-being, you can weather the storms of economic volatility and emerge stronger and more resilient in the face of uncertainty.

# CHAPTER 18: BUILDING FINANCIAL RESILIENCE

Financial resilience is the ability to withstand and recover from financial setbacks, such as job loss, unexpected expenses, or economic downturns, without experiencing significant long-term negative consequences. In this chapter, we'll explore strategies for building financial resilience and strengthening your financial security in an unpredictable world.

# CHAPTER 19: ACHIEVING WORK-LIFE BALANCE

Achieving work-life balance is essential for overall well-being and happiness. In this chapter, we'll discuss practical tips and strategies for balancing your professional responsibilities with your personal life, allowing you to pursue your career goals while prioritizing your health, relationships, and leisure activities.

# CHAPTER 20: EXPLORING ALTERNATIVE INCOME STREAMS

Diversifying your income streams can provide stability and security in an uncertain economy. In this chapter, we'll explore various ways to generate additional income, such as freelancing, consulting, rental properties, online businesses, and passive income streams, allowing you to create multiple sources of revenue and build financial resilience.

# CHAPTER 21: MASTERING NEGOTIATION SKILLS

Negotiation skills are essential for achieving financial success in both personal and professional contexts. In this chapter, we'll discuss effective negotiation strategies, techniques, and tactics that can help you maximize your earning potential, secure better deals, and achieve your financial goals.

# CHAPTER 22: HARNESSING THE POWER OF NETWORKING

Networking is a valuable tool for building relationships, opportunities, and resources that can support your financial journey. In this chapter, we'll explore the importance of networking, practical tips for expanding your professional network, and strategies for leveraging your connections to advance your career and financial goals.

# CHAPTER 23: CULTIVATING A GROWTH MINDSET

A growth mindset is essential for achieving personal and professional growth. In this chapter, we'll discuss the characteristics of a growth mindset, practical strategies for cultivating this mindset, and how adopting a growth mindset can lead to greater resilience, creativity, and success in all areas of your life.

# CHAPTER 24: EMBRACING FAILURE AS A LEARNING OPPORTUNITY

Failure is an inevitable part of the journey to success. In this chapter, we'll explore the importance of embracing failure as a learning opportunity, reframing setbacks as stepping stones to growth and development, and how resilience in the face of failure can lead to greater success in the long run.

# CHAPTER 25:
# CREATING A VISION FOR YOUR FUTURE

Having a clear vision for your future is essential for setting goals and taking proactive steps towards achieving them. In this chapter, we'll discuss the importance of creating a vision for your life, practical exercises for clarifying your goals and aspirations, and strategies for turning your vision into reality.

# CHAPTER 26: OVERCOMING PROCRASTINATION AND TAKING ACTION

Procrastination can be a significant barrier to achieving your goals. In this chapter, we'll explore strategies for overcoming procrastination, increasing productivity, and taking consistent action towards your goals, allowing you to make meaningful progress and achieve success in all areas of your life.

# CHAPTER 27: PRIORITIZING SELF-CARE AND WELL-BEING

Taking care of your physical, mental, and emotional well-being is essential for overall happiness and success. In this chapter, we'll discuss practical self-care strategies, stress management techniques, and habits for promoting well-being and resilience in the face of life's challenges.

# CHAPTER 28: EXPLORING MINIMALISM AND INTENTIONAL LIVING

Minimalism and intentional living focus on simplifying your life, reducing clutter, and prioritizing what truly matters. In this chapter, we'll explore the principles of minimalism, practical tips for decluttering and simplifying your environment, and how intentional living can lead to greater fulfillment and financial freedom.

# CHAPTER 29: PRACTICING GRATITUDE AND MINDFULNESS

Gratitude and mindfulness are powerful practices for cultivating happiness, resilience, and inner peace. In this chapter, we'll discuss the benefits of practicing gratitude and mindfulness, practical techniques for incorporating these practices into your daily life, and how they can positively impact your financial well-being.

# CHAPTER 30: SETTING BOUNDARIES AND SAYING NO

Setting boundaries and learning to say no are essential skills for protecting your time, energy, and resources. In this chapter, we'll explore the importance of setting boundaries, practical strategies for asserting your boundaries effectively, and how saying no can empower you to prioritize what truly matters in your life.

# CHAPTER 31: EMBRACING CHANGE AND ADAPTABILITY

Change is inevitable, and adaptability is essential for navigating life's transitions and challenges. In this chapter, we'll discuss the importance of embracing change, practical strategies for adapting to new circumstances, and how resilience and flexibility can lead to greater success and fulfillment in all areas of your life.

# CHAPTER 32: CULTIVATING HEALTHY RELATIONSHIPS

Healthy relationships are essential for happiness, fulfillment, and overall well-being. In this chapter, we'll explore practical tips for building and maintaining healthy relationships with family, friends, colleagues, and romantic partners, and how nurturing these connections can positively impact your financial and personal success.

# CHAPTER 33: FINDING PURPOSE AND MEANING IN YOUR WORK

Finding purpose and meaning in your work is essential for career satisfaction and fulfillment. In this chapter, we'll discuss strategies for identifying your passions, strengths, and values, practical tips for aligning your career with your purpose, and how pursuing meaningful work can lead to greater financial and personal fulfillment.

# CHAPTER 34: EMBRACING DIVERSITY AND INCLUSION

Diversity and inclusion are essential for fostering creativity, innovation, and success in today's interconnected world. In this chapter, we'll explore the importance of embracing diversity and inclusion in all aspects of life, practical strategies for promoting diversity and inclusion in your personal and professional spheres, and how embracing diversity can lead to greater collaboration and success for all.

# CHAPTER 35: GIVING BACK AND MAKING A DIFFERENCE

Giving back to others and making a difference in the world is deeply fulfilling and meaningful. In this chapter, we'll discuss the importance of philanthropy and community service, practical ways to give back to your community and make a positive impact, and how contributing to the greater good can lead to greater personal and financial fulfillment.

# CHAPTER 36: FINDING BALANCE IN A HYPERCONNECTED WORLD

In today's hyperconnected world, finding balance between work, technology, and leisure is essential for well-being and happiness. In this chapter, we'll explore practical strategies for managing digital distractions, setting boundaries with technology, and creating balance in your life, allowing you to prioritize what truly matters and find greater fulfillment in the digital age.

# CHAPTER 37: PRACTICING FINANCIAL STEWARDSHIP

Financial stewardship involves managing your financial resources responsibly and ethically. In this chapter, we'll explore the principles of financial stewardship, practical tips for managing money wisely, and how adopting a mindset of stewardship can lead to greater financial security, abundance,

# CHAPTER 38: MASTERING TIME MANAGEMENT

Effective time management is crucial for achieving your goals and maximizing productivity. In this chapter, we'll explore practical strategies for prioritizing tasks, minimizing distractions, and optimizing your use of time to accomplish more in less time, allowing you to make the most of every day and achieve your goals with efficiency and ease.

# CHAPTER 39: CULTIVATING CREATIVITY AND INNOVATION

Creativity and innovation are essential for solving problems, generating new ideas, and driving progress. In this chapter, we'll discuss techniques for stimulating creativity, overcoming creative blocks, and fostering an environment that encourages innovation, allowing you to unleash your creative potential and thrive in today's rapidly changing world.

# CHAPTER 40: PRACTICING MINDFUL LEADERSHIP

Mindful leadership involves leading with presence, empathy, and compassion. In this chapter, we'll explore the principles of mindful leadership, practical strategies for cultivating self-awareness and emotional intelligence, and how practicing mindful leadership can inspire trust, foster collaboration, and create positive change in your organization and community.

# CHAPTER 41: NURTURING PERSONAL GROWTH AND DEVELOPMENT

Personal growth and development are lifelong journeys that require commitment, curiosity, and self-reflection. In this chapter, we'll discuss techniques for fostering personal growth, setting meaningful goals, and overcoming obstacles that may stand in the way of your success, allowing you to unlock your full potential and live a life of purpose and fulfillment.

# CHAPTER 42: BUILDING STRONG HABITS FOR SUCCESS

Habits are powerful drivers of behavior and can either support or hinder your progress towards your goals. In this chapter, we'll explore techniques for building strong habits that align with your values and objectives, breaking bad habits, and cultivating routines that support your growth and success, allowing you to create positive change and achieve your aspirations.

# CHAPTER 43: EMBRACING RISK AND EMBRACING FAILURE

Risk-taking is an inherent part of growth and innovation, and learning to embrace risk can lead to greater opportunities and rewards. In this chapter, we'll discuss the importance of embracing risk, managing fear of failure, and reframing setbacks as valuable learning experiences, allowing you to step outside your comfort zone and pursue your boldest aspirations with confidence and courage.

# CHAPTER 44: FINDING JOY IN THE JOURNEY

Life is a journey, not a destination, and finding joy in the journey is essential for happiness and fulfillment. In this chapter, we'll explore techniques for cultivating gratitude, savoring moments of joy, and embracing the beauty of life's ups and downs, allowing you to live with greater presence, appreciation, and contentment each day.

# CHAPTER 45: EMBRACING CHANGE AS AN OPPORTUNITY FOR GROWTH

Change is inevitable, and learning to embrace change can lead to personal growth and transformation. In this chapter, we'll discuss strategies for adapting to change, navigating transitions with resilience and grace, and harnessing the power of change as an opportunity for growth and self-discovery, allowing you to thrive in times of uncertainty and transition.

# CHAPTER 46: BUILDING STRONG RELATIONSHIPS

Strong relationships are essential for happiness, fulfillment, and success in life. In this chapter, we'll explore techniques for building and maintaining healthy relationships, communicating effectively, resolving conflicts, and nurturing connections that bring joy, support, and meaning to your life, allowing you to cultivate fulfilling relationships with family, friends, and colleagues.

# CHAPTER 47: FINDING MEANING AND PURPOSE

Finding meaning and purpose is essential for living a fulfilling and meaningful life. In this chapter, we'll explore techniques for discovering your purpose, aligning your actions with your values and aspirations, and living with intention and passion, allowing you to create a life that is rich in meaning, fulfillment, and purpose.

# CHAPTER 48: CULTIVATING RESILIENCE IN TIMES OF ADVERSITY

Resilience is the ability to bounce back from adversity, setbacks, and challenges stronger than before. In this chapter, we'll discuss strategies for building resilience, cultivating a growth mindset, and developing coping mechanisms that allow you to navigate life's challenges with grace, strength, and resilience, allowing you to overcome obstacles and thrive in the face of adversity.

# CHAPTER 49: PRACTICING GRATITUDE AND MINDFULNESS

Gratitude and mindfulness are powerful practices for cultivating happiness, resilience, and inner peace. In this chapter, we'll explore techniques for practicing gratitude and mindfulness in your daily life, fostering a sense of appreciation, presence, and contentment that allows you to live with greater joy and fulfillment each day.

# CHAPTER 50: LIVING AUTHENTICALLY AND ALIGNING WITH YOUR VALUES

Living authentically means living in alignment with your values, beliefs, and true self. In this chapter, we'll explore techniques for discovering your authentic self, living with integrity and purpose, and making choices that align with your values and aspirations, allowing you to live a life that is true to who you are and what you stand for.

# FINANCIAL TIPS:

- **Start Early:** The power of compounding works best when you start investing early. Even small contributions made consistently over time can grow significantly thanks to compounding returns.
- **Diversify Your Investments:** Spread your investments across different asset classes such as stocks, bonds, real estate, and alternative investments to reduce risk and optimize returns.
- **Stay Informed:** Stay up to date with financial news, market trends, and economic indicators to make informed investment decisions and adjust your strategy as needed.
- **Minimize Fees:** Choose investment vehicles with low fees and expenses, such as index funds and ETFs, to maximize your investment returns over the long term.
- **Emergency Fund:** Build an emergency fund to cover unexpected expenses and financial emergencies. Aim to save at least three to six months' worth of living expenses in a readily accessible savings account or cash reserve.
- **Regularly Review Your Finances:** Periodically review and reassess your financial goals, investment portfolio, and spending habits to ensure they align with your long-term objectives and make adjustments as needed.
- **Plan for Taxes:** Consider the tax implications of your investment decisions and explore tax-efficient strategies to minimize your tax liability and maximize your after-tax returns.

- **Seek Professional Advice:** Consider working with a qualified financial advisor or planner who can provide personalized guidance, expertise, and advice tailored to your unique financial situation and goals.
- **Stay Disciplined:** Stick to your investment plan and avoid making impulsive decisions based on short-term market fluctuations or emotions. Stay disciplined and focused on your long-term financial objectives.
- **Invest in Yourself:** Invest in your education, skills, and personal development to increase your earning potential and expand your opportunities for financial success. Continuous learning and self-improvement are essential for achieving long-term prosperity.

# CONCLUSION: ACHIEVING FINANCIAL MASTERY

In conclusion, mastering your finances is not just about accumulating wealth—it's about cultivating a mindset of abundance, adopting healthy financial habits, and aligning your actions with your values and goals. Throughout this book, we've explored various aspects of personal finance, investing, entrepreneurship, and wealth management, providing insights, strategies, and practical tips to help you navigate the complexities of the financial world and achieve your financial dreams.

Remember that financial success is a journey, not a destination. It requires discipline, perseverance, and a willingness to learn and adapt to changing circumstances. By embracing the principles outlined in this book—such as budgeting, saving, investing, and planning for the future—you can take control of your financial destiny and create a life of abundance, security, and fulfilment.

Whether your goal is to retire early, start a business, travel the world, or give back to your community, financial mastery empowers you to live life on your own terms and make a positive impact on the world around you. So, take the lessons learned from this book, apply them to your life, and embark on your journey towards financial independence and prosperity.

As you move forward, remember that wealth is not just measured by the size of your bank account, but by the richness of your experiences, the depth of your relationships, and the impact you make in the lives of others. Stay true to your values, stay focused on your goals, and never lose sight of the incredible potential within you to achieve greatness.

Thank you for joining me on this journey towards financial mastery. May your path be filled with abundance, success, and fulfilment, and may you always remember that the greatest wealth is found not in what you have, but in who you are and what you contribute to the world.

Here's to your financial success and a life of purpose, passion, and prosperity. Cheers to a brighter future ahead!